PICTURE FACTS

SUN & STARS

N. S. Barrett

Franklin Watts

London   New York   Sydney   Toronto

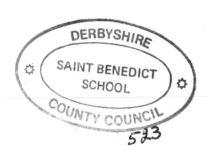

Published by:

Franklin Watts
96 Leonard Street
London EC2A 4RH

Franklin Watts Australia
14 Mars Road
Lane Cove
NSW 2066

ISBN: Paperback edition 0 7496 0648 7
Hardback edition: 0 86313 284 7

Copyright © 1985 Franklin Watts

Paperback edition 1991

Hardback edition published
in the Picture Library series.

Printed in Singapore

Designed by
Barrett & Willard

Photographs by
NASA
Hale Observatories
Schweizerische Astronomische
    Gesellschaft
US Air Force
US Naval Observatory,
    Washington

Illustration by
Janos Marffy

Technical Consultants
Heather Couper
Nigel Henbest

PICTURE FACTS

SUN & STARS

Contents

Introduction

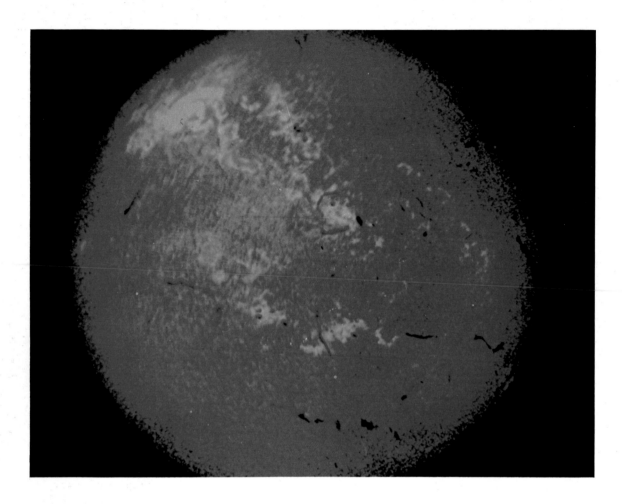

The Sun is the centre of the Solar System. All the planets, including the Earth, revolve around the Sun. It provides us with our light and heat. Without the Sun, there would be no life on Earth.

There are millions and millions of stars in the sky. The Sun is just one of them. It is our star.

△ The Sun is our star. This picture, taken with a special filter, shows its surface clearly. It is a mass of churning hydrogen gas at very high temperatures.

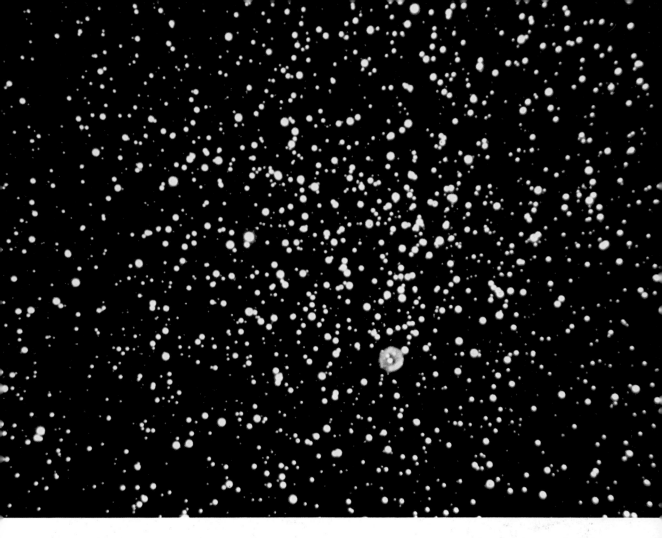

On a clear night, you can see a faint, hazy band of light stretched across the sky. This is the Milky Way, or the Galaxy. With binoculars, you can see that it is made up of millions of stars.

The Sun and all the stars we can see are in our Galaxy. It contains about 100,000 million stars. There are millions of other galaxies.

△ A cluster of stars in our Galaxy. They form just a tiny part of the Galaxy, of which the Sun is an average member.

Our Sun

**Life and death of a star
like the Sun**

2 & 3 The cloud collapses
under its own gravity and
becomes smaller and
hotter

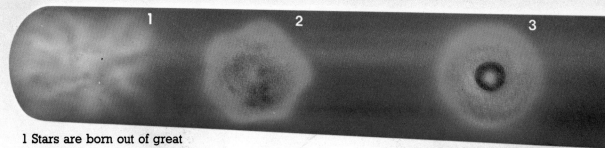

1 Stars are born out of great
clouds of cool gas and
dust

Inside and outside the Sun

— Corona, the Sun's outer
atmosphere

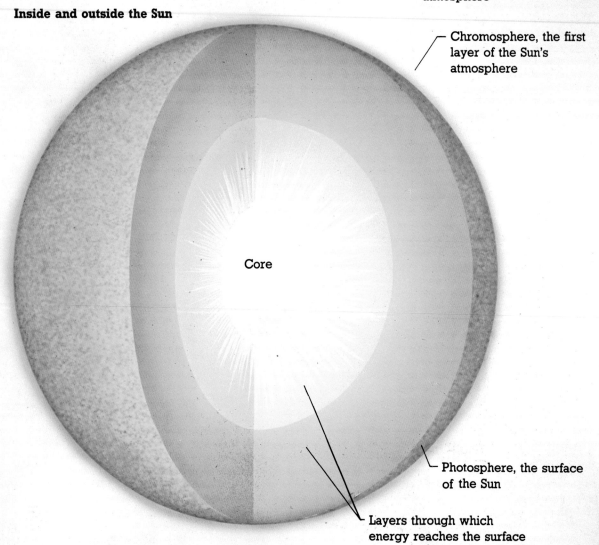

Chromosphere, the first
layer of the Sun's
atmosphere

Core

Photosphere, the surface
of the Sun

Layers through which
energy reaches the surface

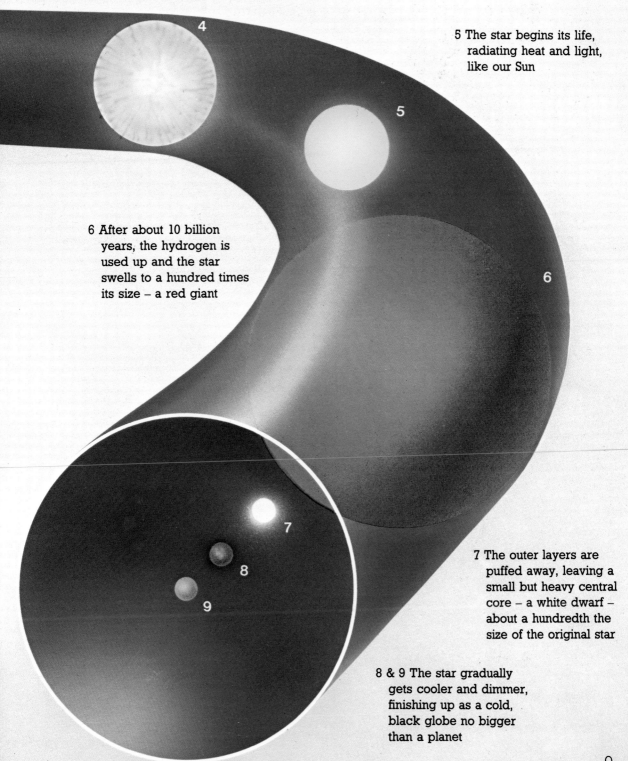

4 The great heat at the centre triggers off the fusion of hydrogen atoms. Energy comes streaming to the surface and stops the collapse

5 The star begins its life, radiating heat and light, like our Sun

6 After about 10 billion years, the hydrogen is used up and the star swells to a hundred times its size – a red giant

7 The outer layers are puffed away, leaving a small but heavy central core – a white dwarf – about a hundredth the size of the original star

8 & 9 The star gradually gets cooler and dimmer, finishing up as a cold, black globe no bigger than a planet

9

Inside the Sun

The inside of the Sun is like a huge furnace. It releases vast amounts of energy in the form of heat and light, and has been doing so for millions of years.

The Sun's fuel is hydrogen, the lightest and simplest substance of all. The energy is produced when hydrogen atoms change into helium, the second lightest substance.

▽ A hydrogen bomb explosion on Earth. In this deadly weapon, hydrogen atoms join up to make helium. In doing so, they release an enormous amount of energy. This is what happens in the Sun.

The Sun's energy is released through its surface into outer space. Sometimes, what look like huge tongues of flame leap out into the Sun's atmosphere.

These are called flares and prominences. Flares are seen as bright flashes of light over wide areas. Prominences are plumes of gas stretching out over vast distances.

△ Massive eruptions on the surface of the Sun shoot out great distances, as can be seen at the top of the picture. About 4 million tonnes of matter in the Sun is converted to energy every second.

11

Studying the Sun

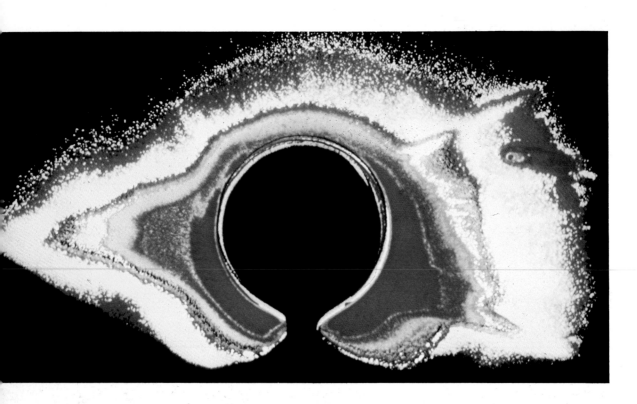

To most people, the Sun rises in the east in the morning, is overhead at mid-day and sets in the west in the evening. It is often hidden by clouds, but we know that it is there. We also know that it is the movement of the Earth that makes the Sun appear to cross the sky.

There is much more to learn about the Sun, however, and scientists spend a lot of time studying it.

△ A special photograph of the Sun taken from Skylab, the American orbiting space station, in 1973. The Sun's disc is blocked out and the Sun's corona may be seen to stretch out into space. The various levels of brightness are shown in different colours.

Scientists learn much during an eclipse of the Sun – when the Moon comes directly between the Earth and Sun and blots out the Sun's disc for a few minutes.

It is only during a total eclipse that the outside layers of the Sun become visible.

▽ The corona as we see it during a total eclipse of the Sun.

The great disturbances seen on the surface of the Sun affect us on Earth. The sunspots, flares and prominences affect our weather and our communications.

△ Giant prominences loop out into space and back again, "steered" by the magnetism of the Sun.

A few years ago a programme was started to study the Sun from space, without the distorting effect of the Earth's atmosphere. Spacecraft with telescopes and other instruments were launched to add to our knowledge of the Sun.

Solar telescopes, those used for studying the Sun, are not like ordinary telescopes. Because the Sun is too bright to look at directly, the image of the Sun is projected on to a screen.

Other special telescopes blank out the Sun's disc. This produces a kind of continual eclipse, to aid study of the Sun's corona.

▽ This special Skylab picture shows a gigantic tongue of energy leaping out from the surface of the Sun.

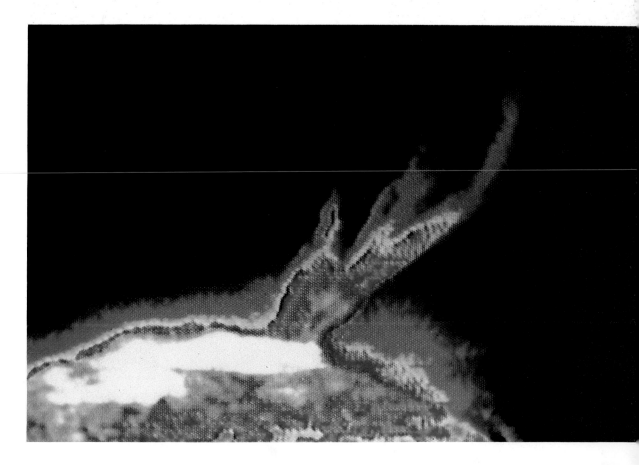

Stars in the sky

On a clear night, you can probably see about 3,000 stars with the naked, or unaided, eye. They appear to differ in brightness. The brightness of a star depends not only on its real brightness, but also on how far away it is.

The Sun is much nearer than any other star. A rocket that took six months to reach the Sun would take over 100,000 years to reach the next nearest star.

▷ The Pleiades cluster is a group of young stars shining with a bright blue light.

▽ The bright star seen here is in the constellation Auriga. Around it are vast clouds of bluish gas caused to glow by the star.

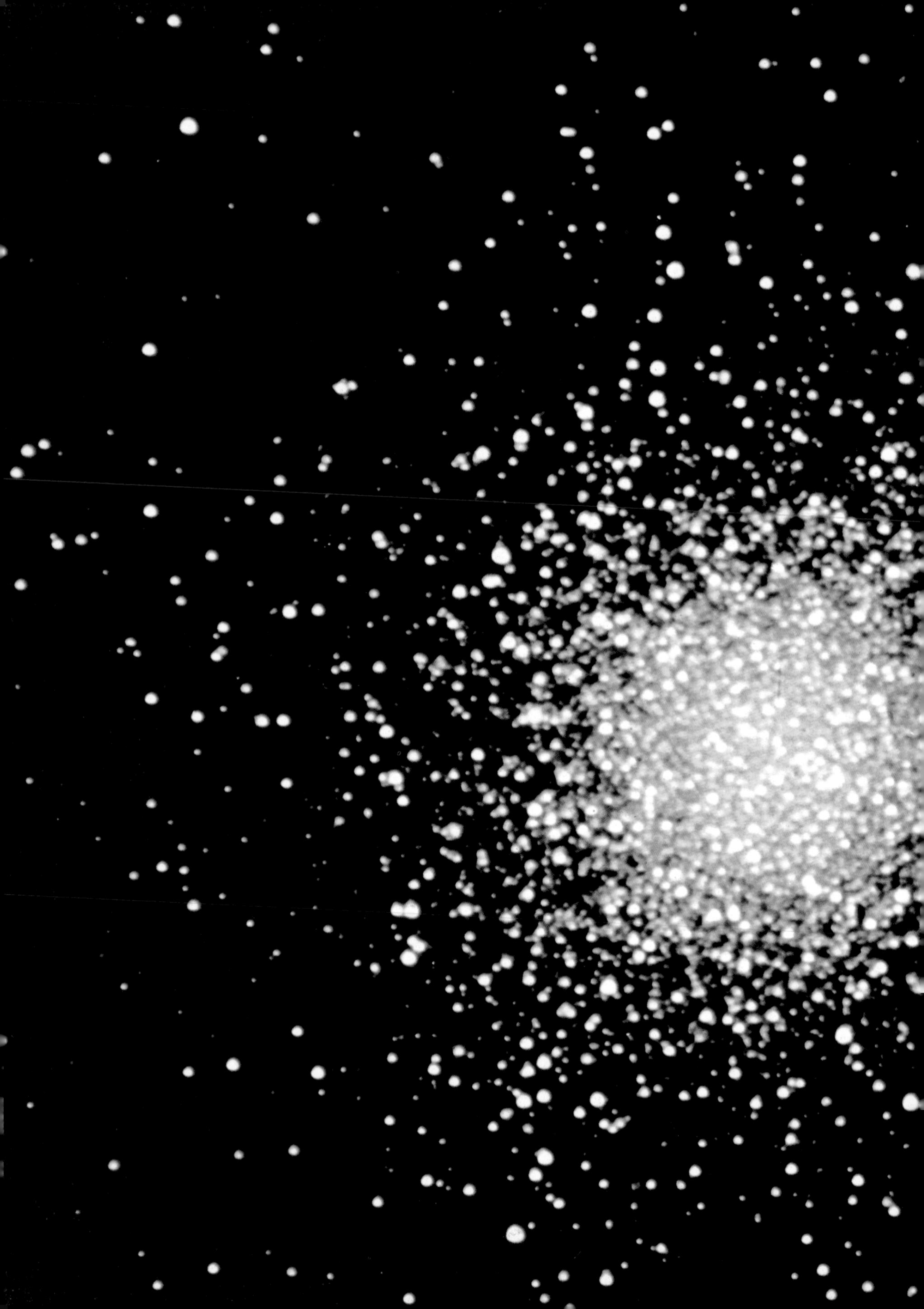

◁ This "ball" of stars is called a globular cluster. It contains hundreds of thousands of stars packed together. Globular clusters are made up of old stars. There are no bright stars in the cluster. To capture the faintest of them in a photograph, the film has to be exposed for one or two hours.

Distance of stars

Light travels at a speed of 300,000 km/sec (186,000 miles/sec). Moonlight takes about a second to reach us on Earth. Sunlight takes just over 8 minutes.

The light from the nearest star takes 4.3 years to reach Earth. We say that the star is 4.3 light-years away. Powerful telescopes can detect stars that are more than 100,000 light-years away.

▽ A distant galaxy may be seen far, far beyond the stars. The stars are less than a hundred light-years away. The galaxy is more than a million light-years away. So we see that galaxy as it was over a million years ago.

Galaxies

Our Galaxy measures 100,000 light-years across. It has the shape of a catherine wheel, with arms that spiral out from the centre. Looked at sideways on, it has a bulge in the centre which is 20,000 light-years thick.

The three main galaxy shapes are elliptical, or oval, spiral and irregular, with no particular shape. Ours is a spiral shape.

△ In the middle of the picture is a spiral galaxy. You can see its arms spiralling out from the centre in all directions.

▷ The central part, or bulge, of the Andromeda galaxy. This beautiful bright glow comes from over 2 million light-years away. The Andromeda galaxy is the farthest object in the night sky that can be seen with the naked eye.

There is another picture of the Andromeda galaxy on page 2, opposite the title page. It was taken over a longer period to show up the spiral arms.

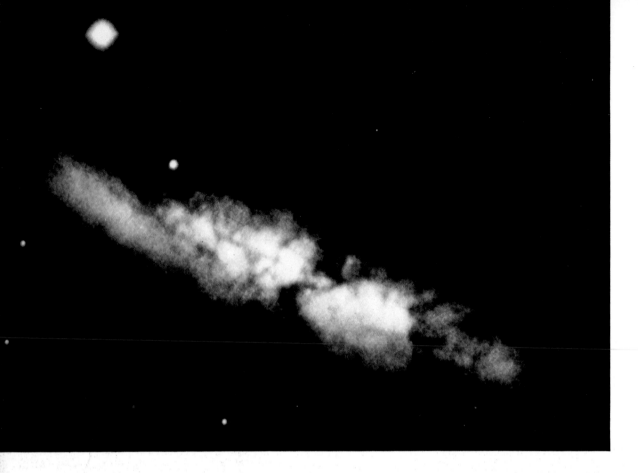

The nearest galaxies to us are the Magellanic Clouds. They are small, irregular galaxies about 200,000 light-years away. The Andromeda galaxy is 10 times as distant. Yet all of these and our Galaxy are in the same group of about 50 galaxies.

There are millions of other groups, or clusters, of galaxies in the universe. The nearest large cluster is 50 million light-years away.

△ An irregular galaxy in the Great Bear constellation, or star group. Vast streamers of hydrogen may be seen moving at high speed, possibly because the galaxy is plunging into a giant gas cloud. Lots of new stars are forming in the galaxy's centre.

Types of stars

Most stars, including our Sun, radiate constant heat and light and are called main sequence stars. They eventually swell up to become red giants, and then shrink to white dwarfs.

Many stars are "twins", or binary stars. They revolve around each other. There are also groups of three or more stars.

▽ After about 10 billion years, stars like the Sun begin to swell up. They eventually become red giants.

Stars differ enormously in both size and weight. A white dwarf might measure only 6,000 km (4,000 miles) across. Some supergiants are 200,000 times as big.

White dwarfs are so dense that a piece of their material the size of a sugar cube might weigh over a tonne. The material in supergiants is light, but some are nearly 10 times as heavy as the Sun.

△ The blue supergiants in this spiral galaxy are thousands of times as bright as the Sun. They light up the clouds of gas within the galaxy.

Exploding stars

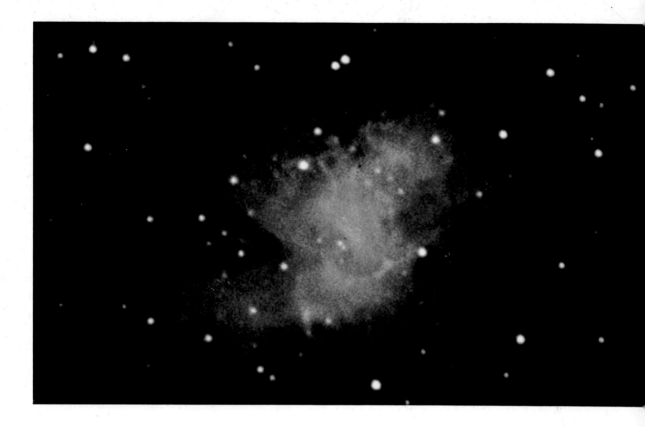

Very massive stars, those 10 or more times as heavy as the Sun, do not just fade away when they die. They explode. An exploding star of this kind is called a supernova.

Supernova explosions occur when the star's hydrogen is used up and the helium is changed into heavier and heavier substances. The explosion gives out more light than a billion Suns.

△ This colourful patch of light in the night sky is called the Crab Nebula. It is the result of a supernova explosion that was seen on Earth in the year 1054. It was so bright that it shone by day for three weeks.

The story of stars

The big bang

The story of the stars began billions of years ago. By studying the Sun and the stars and galaxies, scientists have learnt an amazing amount about how they were formed.

A special method used for studying the stars breaks their light up into a spectrum of colours, like a rainbow. From examining the spectrum, scientists have shown that all the galaxies and groups of galaxies are moving away from each other at enormous speeds. In other words, the universe is expanding. It is thought that all the matter in the universe, everything that makes up the galaxies, began in the same place. There was one tremendous explosion, a big bang as it is called, and matter was sent hurtling into space in all directions.

Even if this theory is right, and most scientists believe it to be so, it does not explain where the matter came from in the first place. That's something we shall probably never know.

Birth of stars

Stars are formed over a period of millions of years, so

△ The Orion Nebula, a great cloud of gas and dust, is lit up by young stars inside it. These were formed from gas and dust and their radiation will drive away the remains of the cloud.

astronomers cannot follow the changes that take place. They have worked out what happens by studying stars in the various stages of their lives.

Stars are made out of huge clouds of gas and dust. This material comes together through the force of gravity. It forms into "globules" that get smaller and hotter. This collapse inwards stops when it becomes hot enough to start up nuclear reactions. These cause great amounts of energy to flow outwards to the surface of the newly formed star. Like the Sun, it then continues to radiate this energy for billions of years.

Stars like the Sun

Stars like the Sun radiate energy for about 10 billion years. After all the hydrogen in the star's core has been used up, gravity takes over again and the core begins to shrink. The outer layers expand and the star becomes a red giant.

A red giant shines brightly, but the outer layers drift off into space like a giant smoke ring in the sky. What's left is a white dwarf star, gradually getting fainter and fainter until it can be seen no more.

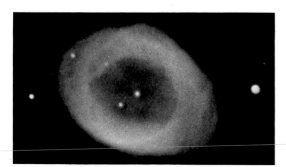

△ The Ring Nebula, the remains of the outer layers of a dying star.

Heavier stars

Stars more than two or three times as heavy as the Sun explode when they near the ends of their lives. Usually they become neutron stars, much smaller even than white dwarfs, perhaps only 25 km (15 miles) across. A pinhead of neutron

△ A mysterious quasar.

star matter would weigh a million tonnes!

A newly formed neutron star spins around very fast. Such stars are called pulsars because they give out pulses of energy.

Black holes

When a giant star explodes and collapses, as in a supernova, the core shrinks so fast because of the great force of gravity that not even light can get out. It becomes what is known as a black hole.

It is thought that black holes might be responsible for the mysterious objects called quasars. These are the farthest objects detected. Some are as bright as a hundred galaxies, yet smaller than the distance from here to the nearest star. Their brightness might be the result of a gigantic black hole at the centre, releasing enormous amounts of energy as matter is sucked into it.

Facts and records

Size of the Sun

The diameter of the Sun is about 1.4 million km (865,000 miles), more than a hundred times that of the Earth. Over a million Earths would fit into the Sun.

Middle-aged Sun

The Sun is an average star and is about half-way through its life. It began shining steadily about 5,000 million years ago and is expected to continue to shine for another 5,000 million years.

△ The Whirlpool galaxy was the first galaxy to be recognized as having a spiral form. There is also a "satellite" galaxy to the right.

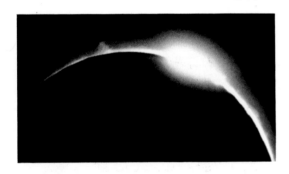

△ A photograph from space of an eclipse of the Sun, taken as its disc is just covered by that of the Moon. There are mountains and valleys on the surface of the Moon. The Sun shining through them sometimes gives the effect of a string of pearls or, as here, a diamond ring.

Sunspots

Patches may often be seen on the Sun's surface which look darker than the rest of it. These are called sunspots. They look darker only because they are cooler than the rest of the surface, about 4,000°C instead of 6,000°C. Some sunspots are as much as ten times the size of the Earth.

Sunspots are due to increased magnetism. They usually last for a few weeks. Every 11 years the number of sunspots reaches a maximum. Sunspot activity tends to interfere with radio communications on Earth.

Nearest star

The nearest star, apart from the Sun, is Proxima Centauri, which is 4.28 light-years away. This is a distance of 40 million million km (25 million million miles).

Glossary

Core
The dense central part of the Sun, where the fusion takes place.

Corona
Outer atmosphere of the Sun.

Eclipse
A solar eclipse occurs when the Moon passes between the Sun and the Earth and blocks out the Sun's light. A total eclipse is when the Moon completely covers the Sun. A lunar eclipse is when the Moon moves into the Earth's shadow.

Flare
An eruption in the Sun's atmosphere.

Fusion
The welding together of atoms, such as hydrogen atoms to form helium, with a violent release of energy.

Galaxy
A vast system of billions of stars and other matter such as gas clouds and dust.

Light-year
The distance light travels in a year.

Milky Way
Our view, from the inside, of our Galaxy.

Nebula
A hazy cloud of gas and dust within a galaxy.

Neutron star
A tiny star which is heavier than the Sun.

Prominence
A streamer of glowing gas hanging above the surface of the Sun.

Pulsar
A rapidly spinning neutron star.

Red giant
A star that has used up its source of energy and whose outer layers have puffed out to make it hundreds of times its previous size.

Solar
To do with the Sun.

Sunspot
A cooler area of the surface of the Sun.

White dwarf
A small dying star.

Index